I0419581

Great Rainforest Facts

Written and Illustrated by:

Amiliyan Love Owens

Copyright © 2015 Amiliyan Love Owens
All rights reserved.
ISBN-13:
978-1514719251

ISBN-10:
1514719258
:

DEDICATION

I dedicate this book to my mother who has always taking care of me.

CONTENTS

ACKNOWLEDGMENTS

I want to thank my teacher Mrs. Maurer's and Miss Huber for their help and my mother for believing in me.

1 THE RAINFOREST

Rainforest can be found all over the world. Some places include Brazil, Belize and Honduras. Rainforest are to the equator where it is hot.

2 THE LAYERS IN THE RAINFOREST

There are four layers in the Rainforest. They are the emergent layer, Canopy layer, Under Story Layer and the Forest Floor Layer.

Plants and animals live in all four layers of the Rainforest.

3 THE CLIMATE IN THE RAINFOREST

The climate in a Rainforest is very warm, wet and humid. Rainforests usually get more than 100 inches of rain in a year.

4 THE RED EYED FROG

The red eyed frog lives in the Rainforest, It can be found in Central America and in Mexico. It can blend in with the leaves by closing its eyes, because it's green eyelids cover it's red eyes.

5 THE ARICAN GREY PARROT

The African Grey parrot also lives in the Rainforest.

You can them in Western and Central Africa and it's very likely that you will see over 100 birds perched in one tree.

6 BLUE MORPHO BUTTERFLY

The Blue Morpho Butterfly also calls the Rainforest it's home. Blue Morpho lives in the tropical forest of Latin America, from Mexico to Colombia. Most of the time they are on the Forest Floor or the Under Story with their wings closed.

7 THE JAGUAR

Another animal you can find the Rainforest is the Jaguar. It lives in Central and South America. It is the largest feline on the American Continent. They eat medium sized mammals, turtles and fish.

8 THE AFRICAN BUSH ELELPHANT

The African Bush Elephant lives in the Rainforest and it is mainly found in Central and Southern Africa.
It eats fruit, branches and grass roots.
They can drink up to 50 gallons of water a day.

9 THE AMERICAN RED START

The American Red Start can be found in the Rainforest. It can be found in Central and Eastern United States and Canada. It eats insects and small fruit. Females have light grey to light green fathers.

10 THE BRAZIL NUT TREE

There are many beautiful plants in the Rainforest. The Brazil Nut tree can be found in the Amazon Rainforest of Brazil. It's height is over 160 feet tall and it weighs over 250 pounds.

11 THE BANANA

The Banana add to the beautiful plant life in the Rainforest. They grow in India, Southeast Asia and Northern Australia. They also can be found in Central and South America. We get most of our bananas from Central and South America.
Without Rainforests, we would not have many things we use everyday such as Ferns, Cut Flowers, Cocoa and Tea. Treat the Rainforest with kindness so that we can enjoy it's beauty.
The End

Some more animals from the Rainforest

ABOUT THE AUTHOR

Amiliyan Owens is 9 years old and lives in Phillipsburg, NJ with her mom, sister, Ta, Brother Tevonne and cousin Hamadi. Amiliyan is a 3rd grade student at Green Street School. She enjoys playing with her friends. She likes helping her mom do the dishes. She also enjoys playing at the park.

www.ingramcontent.com/pod-product-compliance
Lightning Source LLC
Chambersburg PA
CBHW050931290526
45792CB00002B/973